Should Every COMMUNITY Have a Library?

By Mary Austen

Published in 2020 by
KidHaven Publishing, an Imprint of Greenhaven Publishing, LLC
353 3rd Avenue
Suite 255
New York, NY 10010

Designer: Deanna Paternostro
Editor: Katie Kawa

Photo credits: Cover Caftor/Shutterstock.com; p. 5 (top) Rido/Shutterstock.com; p. 5 (bottom) santypan/Shutterstock.com; p. 7 (top) Madhourse/Shutterstock.com; pp. 7 (bottom left and bottom right), 21 (notepad) ESB Professional/Shutterstock.com; p. 7 (inset) PriceM/Shutterstock.com; p. 9 (main) Tyler Olson/Shutterstock.com; p. 9 (inset) In Pictures Ltd./Corbis via Getty Images; p. 11 RobbinsDar/Shutterstock.com; pp. 13 (top), 21 (insets, middle-right and right) wavebreakmedia/Shutterstock.com; p. 13 (bottom) RJ Sangosti/The Denver Post via Getty Images; p. 15 (top) Ermolaev Alexander/Shutterstock.com; pp. 15 (bottom), 17 Rawpixel.com/Shutterstock.com; p. 19 Sylvie Bouchard/Shutterstock.com; p. 21 (markers) Kucher Serhii/Shutterstock.com; p. 21 (photo frame) FARBAI/iStock/Thinkstock; p. 21 (inset, left) Susan Montgomery/Shutterstock.com; p. 21 (inset, middle-left) mattomedia Werbeagentur/Shutterstock.com.

Cataloging-in-Publication Data

Names: Austen, Mary.
Title: Should every community have a library? / Mary Austen.
Description: New York : KidHaven Publishing, 2020. | Series: Points of view | Includes glossary and index.
Identifiers: ISBN 9781534567283 (pbk.) | ISBN 9781534567245 (library bound) | ISBN 9781534531215 (6 pack) | ISBN 9781534567290 (ebook)
Subjects: LCSH: Libraries–Juvenile literature. | Community life–Juvenile literature.
Classification: LCC Z665.5 A99 2020 | DDC 027–dc2

Printed in the United States of America

CPSIA compliance information: Batch #BS19KL: For further information contact Greenhaven Publishing LLC, New York, New York at 1-844-317-7404.

Please visit our website, www.greenhavenpublishing.com. For a free color catalog of all our high-quality books, call toll free 1-844-317-7404 or fax 1-844-317-7405.

CONTENTS

A Changing Role   **4**

More Than Just Books   **6**

Free for Everyone   **8**

Is It Really Free?   **10**

A Safe Space   **12**

A Faster Way to Learn   **14**

Online at the Library   **16**

Not Enough Visitors   **18**

Shaping Your Point of View   **20**

Glossary   **22**

For More Information   **23**

Index   **24**

A Changing
ROLE

Libraries are an important part of many communities. However, their **role** in those communities has changed over time. Now that people can use the internet, they don't always need to go to the library to find **information**. This has caused some people to argue that libraries aren't as important as they once were.

Other people strongly disagree. They believe every community still needs a library because of the important services libraries provide. These different points of view about libraries can **affect** whether or not libraries stay open, so read on to learn more about this **debate**!

Know the Facts!

A recent study found that 95 percent of Americans believe libraries help people learn to love reading.

Should every community have a library now that smartphones can hold more facts than hundreds of books? It's important to answer this question in an informed, or educated, way. This means you need to learn the facts first!

More Than Just
BOOKS

For many years, libraries were known mainly as places where people could borrow books. Then, they also became places to borrow movies, music, and other things to read, watch, or listen to.

Today, libraries are known for much more than the things they lend to patrons—the people who use libraries. They host children's **programs**, book clubs, and movie nights. They're also popular makerspaces, which are places where people can gather to work on crafts or other **projects**. Libraries are great places to learn about and use **technology**, such as computers and 3-D printers.

Know the Facts!

The New York Public Library offers more than 90,000 different programs and events for patrons every year.

A library is much more than just a place to borrow books! There's something for everyone at a library—from crafting classes to homework help.

The New York Public Libray

Free for EVERYONE

Libraries offer most of these services and programs for free, and it costs nothing to visit a library and borrow books. The fact that libraries are free for everyone is one of the most important reasons why people believe every community needs a library.

Books can cost a lot of money, so being able to borrow books for free is very helpful for people who can't afford them. It gives everyone the same chance to learn. Many libraries also offer special help for people who don't always feel welcome other places, such as **refugees**.

Know the Facts!

A group called Libraries Without Borders sets up "pop-up" libraries called Idea Boxes in places around the world where people need help. The people who work for this group believe the free books and services they provide can help people through hard times in their lives.

Librarians are trained to help people find books that are right for them. This includes books about living with disabilities, books about learning English, and books about problems they're facing at home or school.

refugee camp library

Is It Really
FREE?

People don't directly pay to borrow a book from the library or to attend a crafting class there. However, some people argue that the **materials** and services libraries provide aren't actually free.

Libraries get money from taxes, which citizens pay to the government. Many people dislike having to pay a lot of money to the government, and they want to find ways to lower taxes. Some people have argued that one way to cut taxes is to cut the number of libraries. If some communities shared a library, it would cost citizens less money in taxes.

Know the Facts!

In 2018, President Donald Trump called for major cuts to the amount of money given to libraries by the U.S. government. However, the U.S. Congress didn't agree with the president and voted to give libraries more money instead.

It costs money to build a library, fill it with books and other materials, and pay people to work there. This money comes from taxes, which some people feel are too high in their community.

LIBRARY

A Safe
SPACE

Although libraries do need money from taxpayers to stay open, that money helps people who need a safe place to spend time. A library is open to everyone in a community, including people who don't have a home. They can visit a library to get out of the heat or cold. They can also use library services to help them find a job.

Many young people also need a free and safe place to go when they're not in school. They often visit libraries after school, and summer programs at libraries help many kids each year.

Know the Facts!

As of late 2018, around 30 public libraries in the United States have hired social workers to help their patrons. Social workers help homeless people find work, health care, and places to live.

Libraries often serve as safe spaces for people who have nowhere else to go. This is why many people believe libraries need to be a part of every community.

13

A Faster Way
TO LEARN

Many people don't think about the services libraries offer for people who need help. Instead, they only think about the information people get from libraries. They believe this information can now be found on the internet.

For a long time, the library was where a person went when they needed an answer to a question or help with homework. Today, most people can go online to find those things. They can get more information on their smartphone than they can find in all the books in a library. Does this make libraries less important?

Know the Facts!

When American adults were asked about the importance of libraries, 52 percent said the internet has caused them to need libraries less than they once did.

In the past, people went to their local library to look up information and learn new things. Today, they can do this quickly and easily on their computer or smartphone.

Online at the
LIBRARY

Some people believe the internet is **replacing** libraries as a way to get information, but not everyone can get online. People who don't have a computer or smartphone often go to the library to use their computers or internet **access** for free.

Many people, especially older adults, don't know how to do things online. Libraries often have classes that teach computer skills to people who need to learn them. Librarians also answer questions people have about using computers and going online. For example, many librarians help people look for jobs on library computers.

Know the Facts!

A 2016 study showed that the most common reason people used library computers was to look up things for school or work online. People also used library computers to check their email, get health information, and take online classes for school.

Some people believe the internet is a reason people stay out of libraries, but many people actually use libraries to get online!

Not Enough
VISITORS

Most people believe libraries provide important services for the patrons who visit them. However, some people argue that not enough patrons visit libraries to keep them open in every community.

A study of how Americans use libraries showed that only 46 percent of American adults visited at least one library in a year. People who think there should be fewer libraries believe this number shows that fewer people are using libraries now. Because of this, they argue that less money should be spent on building libraries and keeping them open.

Know the Facts!

Adults between the ages of 18 and 35 use libraries more than adults from any other age group. In addition, parents use libraries more than adults who don't have children.

Many people don't know about all the services their local libraries offer. If they don't know all the things they can do at the library, they're less likely to think the library is an important part of their community.

Shaping Your
POINT OF VIEW

A person's point of view is often shaped by their experiences, or the things that happen in their lives. For example, if a person has never gone to a library, they might not believe every community needs one. If a person goes to their local library often, though, they might have a different point of view. People who use a library's many services often believe libraries should be part of every community.

Ask your parent or guardian if you can take a trip to your local library. This can help you decide for yourself if every community needs a library!

Know the Facts!

Around 650 bookmobiles, which are traveling libraries, can be found in the United States today. Bookmobiles give people who can't get to a library building access to important library services, such as the ability to borrow books.

Should every community have a library?

YES

- Libraries provide many important services for free, which means everyone in a community can use them.

- Libraries provide a safe and welcoming place for people who have nowhere else to go.

- People who can't or don't know how to use computers can do this for free at a library.

NO

- Libraries are kept open using money from taxes, and many people don't like to pay a lot of money in taxes.

- People can stay home and get information online instead of going to the library.

- Not enough people use libraries to keep them open in every community.

Even if you don't agree with someone's point of view, it's important to understand why they feel the way they do about an issue such as the importance of libraries. You can use a chart such as this one to see the arguments on both sides of a debate.

GLOSSARY

access: The ability to use or have something.

affect: To produce an effect on something.

debate: An argument or discussion about an issue, generally between two sides.

information: Knowledge or facts about something.

material: Something used during an activity.

program: A set of classes or events related to a certain subject.

project: A planned piece of work that takes time and has a specific purpose.

refugee: A person who has been forced to leave their home country to live somewhere else because their home country is no longer safe.

replace: To take the place of.

role: A part, job, or function.

technology: The method of using science to solve problems. Also, the tools used to solve those problems.

For More
INFORMATION

WEBSITES

ALA: Library Careers for Kids

www.ala.org/educationcareers/libcareers/kids

If you're interested in becoming a librarian when you grow up, check out this part of the American Library Association website.

Ilovelibraries.org

www.ilovelibraries.org

This website offers information for parents and book lovers of all ages about why libraries are important.

BOOKS

Glenn, Sharlee. *Library on Wheels: Mary Lemist Titcomb and America's First Bookmobile*. New York, NY: Abrams Books for Young Readers, 2018.

Harasymiw, Therese. *How Do I Use a Library?*. New York, NY: Britannica Educational Publishing, 2015.

Nugent, Samantha. *Local Library Volunteer*. New York, NY: Av2 by Weigl, 2018.

INDEX

B

bookmobiles, 20

C

classes, 7, 10, 16
computers, 6, 15,
    16, 21

H

homeless people, 12

I

information, 4, 14,
    15, 16, 21
internet, 4, 14, 16,
    17

L

librarians, 9, 16
Libraries Without
    Borders, 8

M

makerspaces, 6

P

patrons, 6, 12, 18
programs, 6, 8, 12

R

refugees, 8, 9

S

safe spaces, 13, 21
services, 4, 8, 10,
    12, 14, 18, 19,
    20, 21
social workers, 12
studies, 4, 16, 18

T

taxes, 10, 11, 21
technology, 6
Trump, Donald, 10

U

U.S. Congress, 10